THE
RONNE EXPEDITION
TO ANTARCTICA

THE
RONNE EXPEDITION
TO ANTARCTICA

by Captain Finn Ronne, U.S. Navy (Ret.)
with Howard Liss

Illustrated with photographs

JULIAN MESSNER NEW YORK

Published by Julian Messner, a Division of Simon & Schuster, Inc.
1 West 39 Street, New York, N. Y. 10018. All rights reserved.

Copyright © 1971 by Finn Ronne and Howard Liss

Printed in the United States of America
ISBN 0-671-32480-2 Cloth Trade
ISBN 0-671-32481-0 MCE

Library of Congress Catalog Card No. 70-161512

Designed by Virginia M. Soulé

*To my daughter Karen who grew up
in an atmosphere of polar exploration, as
did I in my formative years.*

Contents

Chapter

Introduction   9
1 The Expedition is Formed   14
2 Voyage to the Antarctic   25
3 Preparation   35
4 The Long Winter Night   46
5 Exploration—Modern Style   61
6 More Discoveries   79
About Finn Ronne   92
Index   93

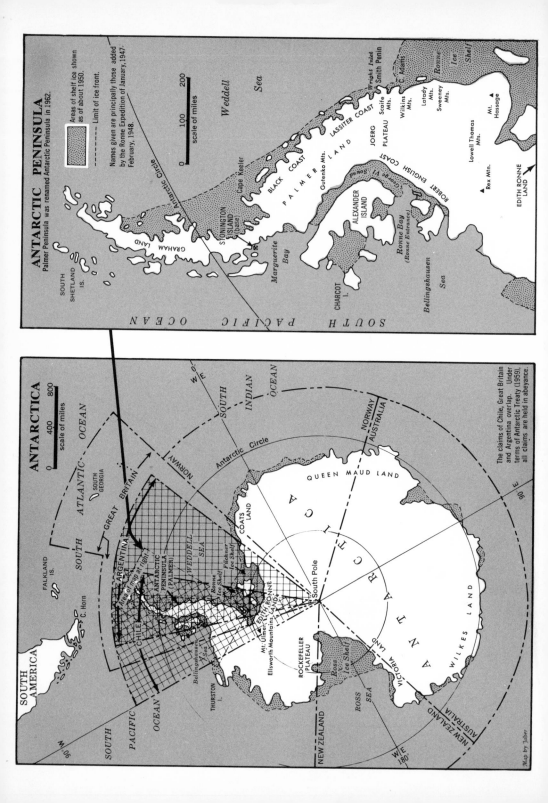

ANTARCTIC PENINSULA
Palmer Peninsula was renamed Antarctic Peninsula in 1962.

Areas of shelf ice shown as of about 1950.

Limit of ice front.

Names given are principally those added by the Ronne Expedition of January, 1947–February, 1948.

0   100   200
scale of miles

Weddell Sea

Wright Inlet
C. Smith Penin.
Scaife Mts.
C. Adams
Wilkins Mts.
Latady Mts.
Sweeney Mts.
Mt. Hassage
Lowell Thomas Mts.
Rex Mtn.
EDITH RONNE LAND
Ronne Ice Shelf

Cape Keeler
BLACK COAST
LASSITER COAST
Gutenko Mts.
PALMER LAND
JOERG PLATEAU
ROBERT ENGLISH COAST

STONINGTON ISLAND (base)
GRAHAM LAND
Marguerite Bay
ALEXANDER ISLAND
(George VI Sound)
Ronne Bay (Ronne Entrance)
Bellingshausen Sea

SOUTH SHETLAND IS.
Antarctic Circle
CHARCOT I.

SOUTH PACIFIC OCEAN

ANTARCTICA

0   400   800
scale of miles

WE

SOUTH ATLANTIC OCEAN

SOUTH INDIAN OCEAN

NORWAY
AUSTRALIA

Antarctic Circle

QUEEN MAUD LAND

The claims of Chile, Great Britain and Argentina overlap. Under terms of Antarctic Treaty (1959), all claims are held in abeyance.

GREAT BRITAIN
NORWAY

SOUTH GEORGIA

FALKLAND IS.
C. Horn

SOUTH AMERICA

ARGENTINA
CHILE
ANTARCTIC PENINSULA (PALMER)

Area of map at right

WEDDELL SEA

COATS LAND

Ronne Ice Shelf
Filchner Ice Shelf

South Pole

90 E

EDITH RONNE LAND
Mt. Ulmer
Ellsworth Mountains

Bellingshausen Sea

THURSTON I.

ROCKEFELLER PLATEAU

Ross Ice Shelf

VICTORIA LAND

WILKES LAND

ROSS SEA

NEW ZEALAND
AUSTRALIA

PACIFIC OCEAN

SOUTH OCEAN

90 W

WIE
180°

Map by Taber

Introduction

Sometimes people ask why anyone would want to explore the Antarctic. After all, no human beings really live there, except for expeditions sent by various governments. Its only inhabitants are seals, penguins, and a few species of birds. As for riches, there are undoubtedly many precious minerals in Antarctica. But they lie buried under a mile of snow and ice, so that it would be almost impossible to do any mining. Then why go there?

Knowledge of the Antarctic is important—very important—if we are to understand fully this planet we call Earth. Many brave explorers have lost their lives trying to find out more about that great white continent.

Only since the beginning of the twentieth century has man really tried to unravel the mysteries of Antarctica. In that short period of time, we have learned much. We have found out about the tides and the temperatures, about the thickness of the ice and the height of the Antarctic mountains. We have studied its earthquake shocks and rock samples. All this information has helped us to understand, in part, how our planet was formed, how it cooled, and perhaps what is in store for us in the centuries to come.

By 1945, when World War II had ended, most of the earth had been explored and mapped. Only one area remained a mystery—the Antarctic. Of the continent's five million square miles, only one third had been explored. There was still much to learn about the vast area at the southern end of the globe.

For example, many geography experts were not sure whether Antarctica was one continent or two. Some thought there might be a strait, covered over with ice, which divided the continent in half. They believed it ran from the Weddell Sea (bordering the Atlantic Ocean) to the Ross Sea (bordering the Pacific).

Perhaps that might not seem very important. After all, what difference does it make if there is a narrow line of water separating the "two Antarcticas"? Especially since the continent is always covered with ice and snow.

But such things can be very important, not only to map makers, but also to nations.

In 1882, a Russian naval officer named Fabian Von Bellingshausen sailed across the sea which now bears his name into the Antarctic. He sighted and marked a strip of land which he called Alexander Land. He thought it was part of the Antarctic mainland. If that was so, then Russia could claim a great deal of territory stretching inland from that small strip of land. For almost sixty years no one disputed Von Bellingshausen's discovery. Everyone took it for granted that Alexander Land was indeed part of the Antarctic continent.

Over the years, many nations, including the United States, sent expeditions into the Antarctic. In 1939, the United States dispatched another crew into the icy wasteland. I was a member of that expedition.

10

Several of us were given the opportunity to explore new sections of the Antarctic. My companion for the trip south was an outstanding dog driver named Carl Eklund. Together we made one of the longest sledge journeys on record. It lasted eighty-four days and covered 1,264 miles.

As we moved south along the western edge of the Palmer Peninsula, we could see Alexander Land. It was separated from the Peninsula by a body of water named George VI Sound. At that time, no one knew how far George VI Sound stretched between the two pieces of land. Eklund and I thought that, sooner or later, we would reach the end of the Sound, where Alexander Land was connected with the rest of Antarctic continent.

Instead, we reached open water! Carl Eklund and I had proved that Alexander Land was an *island,* and not part of the Antarctic mainland. On the basis of that discovery, Russia could not claim large portions of Antarctica after all.

New maps had to be made. They showed that George VI Sound ended in a bay. I named that body of water Ronne Bay, in honor of my father, who had also been an explorer. In addition, a small island was named Eklund Island in honor of Carl Eklund.

That sledge journey across the Antarctic ice had not been my first one. Several years earlier, I had been a member of Admiral Richard E. Byrd's expedition to Little America, which had been Byrd's base camp in Antarctica from 1933 to 1935, and I had driven my dog teams hundreds of miles.

A few weeks before the Byrd expedition was to break

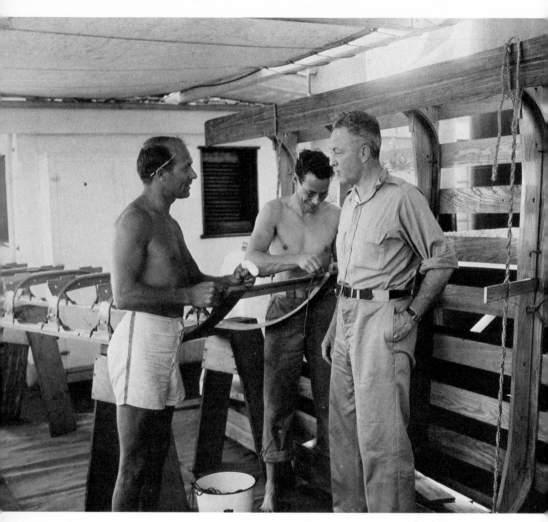

Commander Finn Ronne (left), a dog driver (center) and Admiral Richard E. Byrd (right) stand in front of dog sledges that are lashed together on the deck of the *M. S. North Star*. The ship was crossing the Pacific Ocean from Panama to New Zealand on its way to Antarctica. Ronne was in charge of trail operations during the American government's Antarctic expedition in 1939-41.

camp and leave for the United States, an emergency arose. One of the tractors had broken down many miles from our base camp. Admiral Byrd asked me and two other men to sledge out with some spare parts.

The tractor had broken down not very far from the Rockefeller Mountains. After completing the mission, I sent a radio message back to Byrd, asking if he would allow me to climb to the top of the mountains. Byrd gave his permission. With my two companions, I scaled the heights of Mount Nilsen.

It was then, standing atop that mountain, staring in awe at the great, white barren landscape, that I made a promise to myself. Some day I would command my own expedition into Antarctica.

Years passed before I realized my ambition. The United States became involved in World War II. I enlisted in the navy and rose to the rank of commander. My job was concerned with the ship-building program, and I learned a good deal about many of the smaller ships in the navy. This knowledge proved quite useful later.

During the war, I continued to make plans for my own Antarctic expedition. At last the fighting stopped. And finally, after twelve years of waiting and hoping, my dream came true!

This, then, is the story of the Ronne Antarctic Research Expedition. The United States government gave me some help, but I also had to raise a good deal of money from my friends and from private organizations.

And it turned out to be the last private expedition ever to explore the southern end of our planet.

1

The Expedition is Formed

The Palmer Peninsula, which is part of the Antarctic Continent, lies almost due south of South America's Cape Horn. The peninsula is an icy finger of land, poking up between the Bellingshausen Sea and the Weddell Sea. Drifting fog and clouds, blinding winter blizzards, and constantly blowing winds make it one of the stormiest places on earth.

Even during Antarctic summer, sudden storms rage across the peninsula. No matter what the season, it is safe to fly over the Palmer Peninsula only for short periods of time.

The Weddell Sea, which borders the Palmer Peninsula on the east, is sometimes called "the hellhole of the Antarctic." Because of the extremely cold weather, strong ocean winds, and powerful ocean currents, the Weddell Sea is usually

An aerial view of the Palmer Peninsula showing the mountain ranges
which run up and down the land for hundreds of miles.

choked with pack ice and ice floes.

Half a century ago, explorers found it practically impossible to slice through the ice. Their ships were not strong enough. Even today, modern navy icebreakers have difficulty getting through.

For that reason, even as late as 1945, no one had been able to make an exact map of the Palmer Peninsula coastline, where it bordered the Weddell Sea. That five hundred mile stretch of shore was the last unexplored coastline in the world.

Running up and down the Palmer Peninsula is a mountain range. For a long time, some scientists had suspected that these ice-covered crags were really part of the Andes Mountains of South America. They knew that the rocks of the Andes and those of the Palmer Mountains were quite similar.

Therefore, the scientists thought that the Andes Mountains ran down the western part of South America, continued on under the sea south of Cape Horn, and then rose up again to become the Palmer Mountains.

There were also other mountain ranges farther south of the Palmer Peninsula. Now, suppose the Palmer Mountains were linked up with these mountains to the south? What would that prove?

Well, some other scientists believed that at that point an ice-filled strait cut Antarctica in half. But, if there were mountains in that area, it wasn't possible that a strait would also be there. And if there were linked-up mountain ranges, then Antarctica was one continent, not two.

So my expedition had two missions: First, to make an

Commander Finn Ronne, leader of the Ronne Antarctic Research Expedition (1946-48) is an old hand at Antarctic exploration. His particular mission was to discover and map the unknown interior south and west of the Weddell Sea, make scientific observations and experiments, and prove once and for all whether Antarctica was one or two continents.

accurate map of the Weddell Sea coastline; second, to find out once and for all whether Antarctica was one continent or two.

Today, when the United States government sends a modern expedition into Antarctica, it costs many millions of dollars. A vast amount of equipment must be assembled and shipped there. A thousand or more men conduct the experiments, fly the planes, sail the ships, run the snow cats, repair the machinery, operate the radios. It is truly a tremendous undertaking.

I hoped to raise about $150,000, and thought the missions could be accomplished with about twenty men. Also, a great deal of equipment would be needed.

It was necessary to have a ship large enough to carry the men and equipment. I needed airplanes to fly over the unexplored regions and special cameras to take aerial photographs. There were thousands of items on my lists. Among

them were tractors, food, clothing, coal, tents, stoves, sleeping bags, skis, sledges, Husky dogs, radios, film and developer, cooking gear, compasses, gasoline, medical supplies, and the scientific equipment for various experiments.

Part of the gear could be obtained from government surplus stores. There was an enormous amount of equipment of all kinds crammed into military warehouses. Since the war was over, most of it would never be used. The government was willing to sell a lot of it very cheaply.

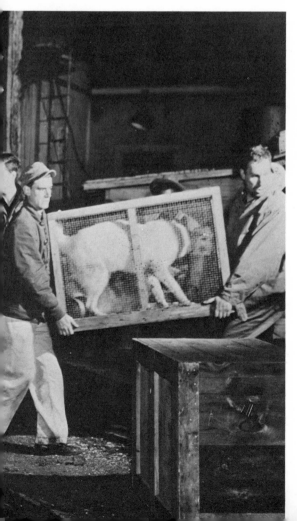

The sledge-dogs arrive at shipside ready for loading. Originating from a kennel in New Hampshire, they had a long train ride to Texas and were brought aboard an hour before departure. Mostly Malamutes, these dogs are natives of Alaska, weigh about 80 pounds, have plenty of proven endurance, and are able to withstand the hardship and cold of temperatures down to 60 degrees below zero (Fahrenheit).

I hoped they would also lend me a ship. Because of my navy work during the war, I knew which ships were no longer being used. I selected an ocean-going tugboat about 183 feet long. It had a wooden hull, two powerful diesel engines, and excellent cargo space.

However, according to federal laws, the navy wasn't permitted to lend a ship to a private individual or an organization, not even for exploration. If I were to get the ship, Congress would have to pass a special law!

Fortunately, I had good friends in the navy. They persuaded some Congressmen to introduce a bill in my behalf. In a few weeks, the bill was passed, and President Harry Truman signed it.

General Curtis LeMay, Chief of Air Corps Research and Development, also helped me greatly. In two weeks, I had three planes and a good deal of additional equipment.

Other help came from the United States Weather Bureau, and from newspaper syndicates which agreed to buy the news stories that I would send from Antarctica. Several of my friends and a number of private organizations contributed some money. I collected about $50,000 in cash.

It was surprisingly easy to enlist men to join the expedition. While Congress was debating whether or not to give me the ship, the newspapers published some stories about the proposed journey into the Antarctic. Before long, I had received more than 1,100 applications! They came from men in all walks of life, from every part of the country.

These men knew I couldn't pay them, but they wanted to join the expedition anyway. In fact, some of them even offered to pay me if I would let them come along. Of course, I couldn't take their money. Besides, I needed men who could be jacks-of-all-trades. They had to be able to help sail a ship, as well as carry out many duties in the Antarctic. After studying the applications, I chose twenty-one men who I thought could do the best job.

Some of the volunteers had served in cold climates before. Commander Isaac "Ike" Schlossbach had been one of the U. S. Navy's first dive-bomber pilots. He was also an experienced navigator. In 1931, when the polar explorer Sir Hubert Wilkins led a submarine expedition under the Arctic ice cap, Ike was the sub's navigator. We were old friends. He and I had been members of the United States Antarctic Expedition of

Some members of the Ronne expedition team. First row, from left to right: Sig Gutenko, Harries-Clichy Peterson, Larry Fiske, and Ike Schlossback. Second row, from left to right: Jim Robertson, Charles Adams, Charles Hassage, Commander Ronne, Mrs. Edith (Jackie) Ronne, and Jim Lassiter.

1939–41. Ike became the skipper of my ship and second-in-command of the expedition.

Our two top pilots were Captain Jim Lassiter and Lieutenant Charles Adams. Both had flown combat missions in all sorts of weather. Harry Darlington, who had also been a navy pilot, was our reserve pilot. Jim Robertson was the aviation mechanic. He turned out to be a wizard at repairing and tuning airplane engines in the bitter cold of the Antarctic.

"Doc" McLean was our medical officer. He had just three months left to serve as an intern before he joined our crew.

Several scientists also volunteered to join the expedition. Bob Dodson and Bob Nichols were both geologists. Andrew Thompson and Harries-Clichy Peterson were brilliant physicists.

Sig Gutenko, the cook had been in charge of ships' galleys during earlier voyages to the Antarctic and to Greenland.

Some others had a great deal of experience in their chosen work. Bill Latady knew just about everything there was to know about photography. Walter Smith had been to sea since he was a young man. During World War II, he had served as an officer aboard a transport ship in the South Pacific. So had Charles Hassage, my chief engineer.

Only in one case did I take a chance on a young, untried volunteer. I received an application from an eighteen-year-old Eagle Scout from Texas. His name was Arthur Owen. There was something so appealing about his letter and his promise to work very hard that I just had to accept him. Arthur lived up to his promise. When the expedition was over, I felt prouder of him than almost anyone else in the crew!

More than a year after I had begun to form the expedition, I learned the ship was ready. It had been refitted at the shipyards in Beaumont, Texas. The workers had toiled long hours to get the vessel in shape. In gratitude, to them and the support given me by the people of the town, I renamed the ship *Port of Beaumont, Texas*.

On January 25, 1947, the *Beaumont* pulled slowly away from the dock. Soon we were on the high seas—destination, the unknown Antarctic.

On January 25, 1947, a fully-loaded *Port of Beaumont* sets sail fom Texas. Her crew, eager to get going, wave farewell from the stern.

All during the time I had been planning the Antarctic journey, my wife Edith (everyone calls her Jackie) had helped me a great deal. She wrote and answered letters, made telephone calls, helped in the purchase of supplies, kept the records, and performed many other duties which made my work easier.

When the ship sailed, I asked her to accompany us only as far as the Panama Canal. When we reached the canal, I persuaded Jackie to stay aboard until we reached Chile. And then she agreed to go all the way to the Antarctic.

Another woman, Jennie Darlington, the wife of our reserve pilot, also went along. These two became the first women ever to spend an entire winter in the Antarctic.

2

Voyage to The Antarctic

Any man who commands an expedition is faced with a great challenge and many difficulties. He is responsible not only for the success or failure of his mission but also for the lives of his men. If the mission is successful and all the men return safely, he takes a good share of the credit. But if the expedition fails, or if some of the men are injured or killed, then he must take the blame, even though he might not have been at fault.

In the Antarctic, dangers are always present. The men had to be warned in advance about the risks they would face. Their enemies would be the cold, the crevasses, and one of nature's strangest tricks, the whiteout.

The Antarctic is the coldest region on earth, far colder

Antarctica's terrain, broken by jagged mountains with peaks over 10,000 feet high, flat plateaus of icy snow and impassable glaciers, is beautiful to see—but deadly to the courageous men seeking to probe its secrets.

than the Arctic. Even at the North Pole, temperatures seldom drop lower than 60 degrees below zero Fahrenheit. The Antarctic has registered temperatures of 120 below zero—and even colder. During my first trip to the Antarctic with Admiral Richard E. Byrd in 1933, I sledged across open snow fields while the wind howled and the thermometer plunged to 65 degrees below zero!

The United States Army has done much research on the effects of cold and wind on the human body. They have formed what is called the 30-30-30 rule. When the temperature drops to 30 degrees below zero, and the winds blow at 30 miles an hour, exposed human flesh can freeze in 30 seconds.

Crevasses are another terrible danger. These cracks in the ice and snow can be very narrow or very wide. Often there is no way to know in advance where they are. Usually, the crevasses are covered by a "bridge" of snow. Many times I have poked my ski poles into innocent-looking snow, and seen huge holes open up almost under my feet. Several experienced explorers have lost their lives when they were swallowed up in crevasses which were more than two hundred feet deep.

Crevasses are one of the terrible dangers always present in the Antarctic. This aerial view of a crevasse field shows the many breaks in the ice and snow, which present hidden dangers to explorers. Usually, the crevasses are covered by a "bridge" of snow, and so there is no way to know in advance where they are. Some crevasses are more than 200 feet deep.

· When Carl Eklund and I sledged across the Palmer Peninsula, we encountered numerous crevasses. A few times we had narrow escapes.

We never fell into a hole, but the dog team did. When only the Huskies slid into the hole, it wasn't difficult to stop the sledge and haul the dogs back to safety. But on one occasion, when we crossed a strong snow bridge, the dogs reached the other side safely; the heavy sledge, with its half-ton of supplies broke through the bridge and started to slide slowly into the darkness below.

The Huskies felt themselves being dragged backward into the gaping hole. Instinctively, they dug their paws into the snow, slowing the fall of the sledge. Quickly, Eklund and I began to hammer "dead men"—wooden poles—into the ice near the sledge runners. The sledge hung on the lip of the crevasse, teetering dangerously.

Even with the help of the powerful Huskies, Eklund and I could not drag the heavy sledge back to firm ice. First it had to be unloaded. I tied a rope around my waist, climbed slowly down on the sledge and began to unpack the bags of supplies. One by one I handed them up to Eklund.

As I fumbled with knots and ropes, I tried not to look down into the blackness below, for that would make me dizzy. It was something like working atop a tall skyscraper, and leaning over the edge all the time. Only the rope prevented me from plunging hundreds of feet to my death. And, through all the hours Eklund and I toiled, the frigid winds numbed our fingers and cut through our fur clothing.

28

Commander Finn Ronne (left) and Carl Eklund (right) had many close calls during their 1,264 mile journey across the Antarctic. Once a fully-loaded sledge, like the one behind them, fell into a crevasse and nearly dragged their dog team to its death.

Finally, when the last bag was unloaded, I climbed up again. The dogs, Eklund, and I all tugged hard at the sledge and hauled it back to safety. Then the supplies were reloaded, and the journey continued.

A whiteout can best be described as a combination of being partly blind and also seeing mirages. It is like being surrounded by a sea of absorbent cotton. Everything looks blurry and white as if one were marooned in a dense fog. A whiteout is caused by the glare of the sun, as it bounces off the white snow and strikes the eyes. A person who is experiencing a whiteout *thinks* he can make out familiar objects, but really he can't. A piece of ice, only a few yards away, seems to be a large hill of ice several miles in the distance. There is only one way to overcome a whiteout, and that is to stay perfectly still and wait patiently until it passes. Generally that doesn't take too long.

These are the *physical* dangers of the Antarctic. But there is a greater peril—*panic*.

In many difficult situations, calm thinking can overcome even hopeless odds. But when a person in trouble loses control and begins to run blindly, not knowing where he is going or what he will do next, he faces sudden death. As commander of the expedition, I warned my crew against panic.

For weeks the *Beaumont* sailed peacefully over the Atlantic Ocean, then through the Panama Canal and out into the Pacific. Then, suddenly, the Huskies were hit by an epidemic of distemper, which is a deadly viral disease affecting animals, especially dogs.

Huskies can withstand incredible cold. They love freezing weather, they thrive in it. But they can become sick if exposed to hot, muggy weather for long periods of time.

The older dogs had been given shots to prevent distemper, but not the smaller, younger dogs. There was no distemper vaccine on the ship, nor was there any in Valparaiso, Chile, where the ship docked for a time. Some of the Huskies died. When the *Beaumont* reached cooler latitudes, the distemper epidemic was over.

30

As the ship sailed deeper into Antarctic waters, huge icebergs came into view. Only about 10 percent of an iceberg shows above the water line, but the towering masses of ice looming up in front of us were as tall as office buildings. Many were as wide as several city blocks. Antarctic icebergs can be fantastically large. A few have been measured at *220 miles across!*

Huge towering icebergs—some as wide as several city blocks—are broken from glaciers by their own weight and the motion of the sea. The largest iceberg was sighted in 1931. It measured 275 feet above the water line and was 34 miles long.

Finally, the Antarctic continent itself was sighted. There are few sights in the world more spectacular than the massive ice cliffs which ring much of the continent.

These ice cliffs, which rise up along the shore about 150 feet high, are really the edges of huge glaciers. The glaciers are formed miles away, deep in the interior of Antarctica, in the high ground. They move slowly down from the plateaus and mountains toward the shores of the seas. Every so often a great chunk of ice cliff will break off, just as though a huge axe had chopped it away. The chunk floats out to sea in the form of an iceberg.

It is impossible to moor a ship along one of these ice cliffs. There is simply no place to land. Besides, there is always the danger that a piece of the glacier will break off and smash the ship to bits.

That was one important reason for choosing Stonington Island, in Marguerite Bay, as the main base for the Ronne expedition. Stonington Island is one of the few places in the Antarctic where the land slopes gradually out to sea. Equipment could be taken from the ship and moved right onto the land.

There were other good reasons for choosing Stonington Island. The island is very close to the Palmer Peninsula, which we intended to explore. Only a glacier about 100 yards long separated the island from the Palmer Peninsula.

The old base camp, which I had helped to build for the United States Antarctic Expedition, was still on Stonington Island. When I had left the camp, less than six years before, it

Upon its arrival at Stonington Island, the expedition ship is surrounded by drifting pack ice. To the left is Neny Island, an easily recognizable landmark. It was especially useful to the flight crews when they returned from their flights into the unknown.

was in very good condition. I intended to use it again for my expedition.

There was also a British base on Stonington Island, about half a mile from the old base camp. Actually, England, Chile, and Argentina all laid claim to Stonington Island and the Palmer Peninsula. The United States did not recognize these claims, and insisted that the region must be open to all nations for exploration.

Major Butler, the commander of the British base, told us that some navy ships from Chile and Argentina had visited the island. The sailors had broken into our buildings, smashed some of the things that had been left behind, and helped themselves to whatever they thought might be useful.

It was mid-March, almost the end of Antarctic summer. Soon the winter night, with its bitter cold, high winds, and howling blizzards would close in. We couldn't use the old camp until it was repaired. The buildings had to be patched, the walls sealed, the floors fixed. And it had to be done quickly.

3

Preparation

Many people have the wrong idea of what happens at the beginning of an expedition. Perhaps they have seen too many adventure movies: The hero and his friends get off the ship and go dashing out to explore distant mountains and valleys.

But most expeditions aren't that exciting, at least not in the beginning. The first part of an expedition usually consists of doing two things: preparing men and equipment, and then waiting for the right time to move out.

We had reached Antarctica only a few weeks before the start of winter's freeze. That might seem strange. Why didn't we get there just before the start of Antarctic summer? Then we could get ready quickly and begin to explore at once.

Actually, we were not yet prepared to go anywhere. Even though we had not expected the old base to be in such

Shortly after their arrival, Commander Ronne (third from left) with the members of his team raised the American flag over Stonington Island.

poor condition, there was a great deal of work to be done before a single dog team could be sent out to probe the secrets of the Antarctic.

The ship had to be unloaded.

All the supplies had to be stored.

The scientific gear had to be made ready for use.

The crew had to stow their personal things and make themselves snug and comfortable.

The dogs had to have special quarters.

Trail food had to be prepared and frozen.

The base camp had to be repaired.

The expedition suffered yet another disappointment. I had planned to send a sledge party to the southern end of the Palmer Peninsula's mountain range when summer came. But that was a very long journey. The sledgers would need plenty of supplies, far more than one team of dogs could drag. I had hoped to sail the *Beaumont* through George VI Sound for about three hundred miles, drop off a cache of food and equipment, mark the spot well, and then return to our base on Stonington Island. In that way, my sledge drivers would have enough food and gear for the journey.

Harry Darlington, the reserve pilot, took off in the light scout plane to check the waters of George VI Sound. He returned in a few hours with bad news. The sound was full of huge icebergs. The *Beaumont* would never get through.

We tried anyway. But after a few miles, I realized that it was impossible. The icebergs were everywhere. Besides, it was getting colder and colder. If the temperature dropped swiftly, the *Beaumont* might be stuck in the ice far from Stonington Island. We turned back. The supplies would have to be dropped off later by an overland route.

Meanwhile, my crew was working hard, repairing the old camp and building a few other small buildings, before the cold weather would set in.

Living quarters had to be finished before the cold weather set in. Two men bunked in one cubicle: in the lower bunk, Charles Hassage, and in the upper bunk, Bob Dodson.

Andrew Thompson, the physicist, built a shelter for his sensitive instruments. Here he is studying recordings of earthquakes obtained by a seismograph.

Andrew Thompson, one of the physicists, had never before tried to do carpentry work. Yet he succeeded in building a shack for some sensitive instruments. The instruments measured the tides, the tremors of the earth's crust, and the magnetic fields of the Antarctic.

Harries-Clichy Peterson, the other physicist, also built a shack. This one became a weather station. He sent up balloons and was able to measure air currents by how fast the balloons went up and in which direction they flew.

Bob Dodson, a geologist, had volunteered to test some of the army's field equipment. He slept outside in some new-style tents and sleeping bags. After several very uncomfortable nights, Dodson found that they weren't very good. The zippers got stuck, too much cold air seeped through the cloth, and the bags weren't warm or waterproof.

Nelson McClary, the second mate, was almost killed trying to erect the radio antenna.

Because it was getting very cold, the men who were working outside wore fur parkas. The wind was cold and strong, so McClary wore the hood of his parka over his head and ears to keep warm. He was walking backward, unspooling some wire from a roll, and he didn't hear the warning shouts of his fellow workers. McClary kept walking backwards, and suddenly he dropped over the edge of a sixty-foot ice cliff!

Horrified, the rest of the men raced to the edge of the cliff and looked down. They saw that McClary had fallen through a two-inch layer of ice and was floundering helplessly in the water.

At Stonington, the men worked in bitter cold to string the wires of the radio station. It was this cold that nearly killed Nelson McClary when his protective clothing blocked the shouted warnings from his friends and he backed over a cliff.

There was no time to climb down for the rescue, for by that time McClary would have drowned. Jim Robertson, the mechanic, realized instantly that McClary had to help save himself.

Robertson hitched a long coil of climbing rope to a tractor, and dropped the other end to McClary. It splashed into the water right near him. He was in terrible pain, but somehow he managed to tie the rope around his chest. The tractor lurched forward and McClary was hoisted back up to the top of the ice cliff.

Hot-water bottles were placed carefully over McClary's ribs, chest, and back. Members of the crew took turns gently rubbing his arms and legs to get the blood circulating again. But they had to be careful not to touch his fingers or toes. His skin peeled in several places, and for weeks he was stiff and sore. But at last he recovered and went back to his duties.

The *Beaumont* was put in mothballs. That is to say, it was allowed to freeze fast into the ice. All the metal on the ship was coated with grease or graphite to prevent it from rusting. All the hatches were sealed, all the air ducts were closed tightly. The radios were stored away so that moisture would not damage the insides.

Some of the men went seal hunting. This was not done for sport, but because seal meat and seal blubber were important for the Huskies' diet. It was part of their trail food.

Long ago, explorers learned that food had to be concentrated if it was to be used in the Antarctic snows. Dogs could not drag too much weight. Therefore, each bit of food, for dogs or humans, had to be special in its own way. It had to be more nourishing than ordinary foods found in the home, yet light in weight. Also, dogs and men needed lots of fat in their diet in order to do the work and remain healthy.

Sig Gutenko, the cook, prepares the mixture of soy meal, bacon fat, barley, wheat germ and bits of meat, known as pemmican.

"Man food" was a kind of pemmican which had the right combination of protein, carbohydrates, vitamins, and minerals to keep hard-working men in good health while on the trail. It consisted of soy meal, bacon fat, barley, wheat germ, bits of meat, and several other ingredients. This mixture was formed into blocks and left outside to freeze.

On the trail, the blocks of pemmican were shaved into some water and heated over a small cook stove. We used Primus stoves, which burned kerosene. The food tasted something like greasy hamburger soup, but it was warm and filled the stomach.

There was also some chocolate, tea, cookies, and other foodstuffs in each bag of supplies.

"Dog food" might be just a pound-and-a-half chunk of seal meat. Or it might consist of commercial dog meal mixed with melted seal blubber. This mixture was also formed into blocks and left outside to freeze.

The Huskies ate their food with astonishing speed. One or two hard chomps with their sharp teeth and the blocks of food were gone.

At the beginning of May, I decided to have a party for

Many litters of pups were born during the dark winter-night. To protect mother and pups, they were always given special treatment and housed in the storeroom where they were protected from the elements. The other dogs were chained in snowy tunnels outside. Commander Ronne is seen here feeding his favorite puppies.

the crew. They had worked hard and deserved it. Sig Gutenko cooked a chicken dinner, and the sight of the chickens was greeted with loud cheers by the men. No, the crew had not been starving—far from it. They were simply sick and tired of eating steaks all the time!

The Antarctic does peculiar things to a man's appetite. Because of the hard work and the constant cold, the men always ate lots of food, and the fatter the food, the better they liked it. Good steak is tasty, but it is lean meat. Plump chickens have some fat under the skin, and the men liked that. They even liked hamburger better than steak, because the ground beef had fat.

The men also wanted a great deal of starch and sugar, especially chocolate candy. The sugar was really ready energy. Having spent two winters in the Antarctic, I knew that would happen. Among our supplies was more than three thousand pounds of chocolate candy. The crew also had plenty of bread, cakes, and pies.

Soon winter was upon us. By now the buildings were snug and comfortable, the supplies safely stored. Darkness covered the great white Antarctic continent.

Before the coming of the long winter darkness that blanketed the Antarctic continent, the members of the expedition worked very hard to store their supplies and make the buildings as snug and comfortable as possible.

4

The Long Winter Night

The seasons in the southern hemisphere are the exact opposite of those in the northern hemisphere. For example, when it is winter in North America, it is summer in South America, Australia and the Antarctic. Therefore, winter in Antarctica comes in the middle of June.

By the middle of May, the Antarctic sun no longer climbs over the horizon. For a couple of weeks it is like twilight or sunset. The sun's rays shoot up into the sky, turning it orange or red. The rays bounce off the clouds, turning them into rainbow-colored cotton candy—oh, so very beautiful! Gradually twilight grows shorter and shorter, until at last there is no sunlight at all and the long winter night sets in.

But the skies are not completely dark. Millions of stars are sprinkled across the heavens, and they seem larger and brighter than ever. The moon seems to have an especially bright quality too.

And the southern lights are breathtaking! Curtains of colors streak across the sky: fire-red, orange, and yellow. The sheets of colors dance and swirl, zigzagging in fantastic patterns. There is no way to describe their awesome beauty. One can see the lights a thousand times and find that they are always different, always more dazzling than the last time.

Winters are extremely cold. Of course, there are places in the United States which are about as cold as Stonington Island. For example, at International Falls, Minnesota, which is on the Canadian-American border, sometimes the temperature drops to 40 or 50 degrees below zero. But that doesn't happen very often. In Antarctica, such low temperatures are quite normal during the winter.

When the darkness closed over our camp, the men had finished nearly all their work. There wasn't much for them to do, but they kept busy in a number of ways. They melted ice for fresh water, helped in the kitchen, or hauled some additional supplies from the ship to the camp. Equipment was checked and made ready for use in spring and summer. Some scientific experiments were performed: weather records were kept, as well as records of the winds and thickness of the ice covering the waters of George VI Sound.

The two ladies had plenty to keep them occupied. My wife Jackie kept the log, a complete account of the expedition's activities, and typed out all my reports. She helped Andrew Thompson, the physicist, with the readings of the seismographs and the tidal station. During the summer, when Thompson was out in the field, Jackie operated these scientific instruments and kept them in good working condi-

Harries-Clichy Peterson measures the speed of the wind with an anerometer. To protect himself from high winds of over 100 mph, he invented a plastic shield which also allowed him to see what he was doing.

Lawrence Kelsey, radio operator, sent scientific results and news stories to the outside world.

Arthur Owen (left) and Nelson McClary (right) splice gang-lines and traces of rope for the dogs and sledges.

tion. Mrs. Darlington was also very busy. She catalogued the 3,000 books which formed the expedition's library. Later, she helped photographer Bill Latady develop his film and make prints.

The rest of the time everyone watched movies, listened to records, or worked on hobbies, such as wood carving or metal crafts. A few of the men studied navigation or practiced sending and receiving messages by radio.

Meanwhile, as commander of the expedition, I had began planning exactly how and when we would begin to explore the Palmer Peninsula. Of course, many plans had already been made, even while we were at sea. Now those plans had to be put into operation, and it had to be done one step at a time.

For example, one of our most important missions was to explore the *eastern* coast of the Palmer Peninsula, where it bordered the Weddell Sea. But our base camp was near the *western* coast of the peninsula. That meant, we would have to establish an advance supply base on the eastern coast. Supplies would have to be flown across the mountain range which ran down the middle of the peninsula.

But that was not as simple as it sounds. It was very difficult to know what kind of weather we would encounter. We might be enjoying fair skies at Stonington Island, but over the mountains and beyond a blizzard might be raging. What if the storm clouds were too high for our supply planes to fly over? There was great danger of a crash—men killed, supplies lost, the whole mission in peril of failure.

But a weather station could warn us of approaching storms. Having sledged on the Palmer Peninsula before, I knew just where such a station should be established: on a high plateau along the edge of the mountains. From there, the men at the station could radio back to base and tell us when the weather was suitable for flying.

The weather station would be nothing more than a tent in which two men, Bob Dodson and Harries-Clichy Peterson, would work and live. Their gear would include a radio, a number of weather balloons and instruments, and plenty of food.

A party of six men. myself included, and two dog teams set out in mid-July. It was a rugged trip. Covering the twenty miles to where the weather station was to be set up took two days of hard sledging. We struggled up the slopes of the plateau, and every step was difficult. When the dogs could no longer advance the sledges, we worked out a new way to move ahead. We attached both dog teams to one sledge, then helped them drag the half-ton of supplies to the top of a ridge. The

dogs were unhitched, then the second sledge was dragged up the same way.

Everywhere, whether on a slope or flat ground, we encountered dangers. On the slopes, we were narrowly missed by several avalanches, which roared down the steep grades. The flat sections were honeycombed with crevasses. Some opened up under the probing of my ski poles, others were in plain view, and we had to go around them.

At last we reached our destination. Suddenly, almost without warning, a blizzard struck furiously. Just minutes after we had stopped the sledges, the winds were howling and the snow was beating at us. Somehow we managed to get the tents set up, although they almost blew away any number of times. The dogs were tethered to steel cables. As soon as everything was secure, the men dived inside the tents.

We all breathed a sigh of relief. Outside, a man would

After a long day of hard pulling in harness, the dogs are chained on a tethering line. They watch the drivers' every move and wait especially for their cake of dog food—their daily reward.

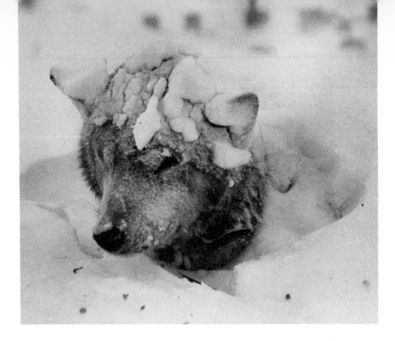

The dogs did not mind being buried in snow. They simply curled up—snug and comfortable—flipped their bushy tails over their noses, and had no trouble breathing beneath a layer of snow.

die in an hour if he was without shelter; yet, in our tents we were snug. The snow covered the tents, the dogs, and the equipment.

The dogs didn't mind being buried in the snow. They simply curled up, flipped their bushy tails over their noses, and in a short time were fast asleep. They had no trouble breathing beneath the layer of snow.

For five days the storm raged. The wind gusted up to almost ninety miles an hour, and sometimes it seemed that our tents would be swept away, and us with them. At last the winds died down. The sheets of snow turned into a mere drizzle of flakes, and finally stopped falling. The skies were lighted by a flood of stars.

The weather station was now ready to operate and we prepared to leave. It was decided that Dodson and Peterson did not need a sledge or dog team. Since both could ski fairly well, if they had to they could return to the base on skis.

The trip back to the base on Stonington Island was very easy. It was all downhill. We had taken two days to cover those twenty miles to the plateau. Our homeward journey took only eleven hours.

The next day we received our first message from the weather station. The spotters reported high winds buffeting the plateau again. The winds were so strong that both men could hardly venture out of the tent. And that was the last message we received from Peterson and Dodson.

For four days there was nothing but silence from the weather outpost. We tried calling them by radio, but there was no reply. The foul weather had also covered Stonington Island,

A roaring blizzard hit the Ronne expedition base on Stonington Island and knocked out all radio communications. During this blizzard, a wind speed of 87 miles an hour was recorded for five minutes, with gusts of as much as 110 miles per hour.

so that the scout plane could not be sent up to see what had happened.

Suddenly the skies cleared. The small plane was promptly dispatched to the plateau. It flew low over the tent, but no one came out to signal to the plane.

Hearing this disturbing news from the pilot, I began to assemble a relief party. But before the sledges could move out, Bob Dodson came staggering into the main bunkhouse. He was exhausted and terrified. He told this story:

The day after we left the weather station, a new storm began to whip the tent. The cloth began to sag and rip under the weight of the snow and the force of the winds. The two men decided that anything was better than remaining in that howling blizzard with a torn tent. They would make a run for it, back to the base.

Dodson and Peterson were only halfway back when they got lost. Crevasses were everywhere. They poked their way ahead, cautiously, thinking that soon they would be clear of the crevasse-field. When they thought all danger was past, they took off their skis.

That was the worst thing they could have done. At least the skis offered some protection against falling into an unseen hole.

They pushed on, battling the screaming winds and stinging particles of snow. Suddenly, Peterson disappeared! He had vanished into a crevasse.

Dodson crept to the edge of the hole and called down. Peterson answered that he was all right but needed a knife.

54

Dodson lowered a knife at the end of a rope but Peterson didn't take it, and not another sound was heard from him. Not knowing what else to do, and realizing that he was doing no good by himself, Dodson decided to go on alone. He marked the spot by sticking his skis into the snow, then continued toward the base. He staggered ahead blindly, praying that he too would not plunge into a hidden crevasse.

Less than an hour after Dodson reached Stonington Island, a rescue party was on its way back toward the plateau.

We had to be careful because of the crevasses, yet we also had to move fast if we were to help Peterson at all. Powerful flashlights were kept shining, moving from one place to another. In that way we were able to avoid at least a dozen open pits in the snow.

But we weren't so lucky. Once, two dogs broke through a snow bridge and were dangling by their harnesses. One dog was pulled to safety, but the other one kept working his jaws savagely in fright. He chewed through his harness and dropped to his death in the deep pit.

Finally we reached the area where Dodson thought he had left his skis. But it wasn't so easy to find them. It took us three hours to find the skis which were near the crevasse where Peterson was a prisoner. We crawled to the edge and looked down. It wasn't too deep a hole, so Peterson could not have fallen very far. One of the smallest men in the rescue party—his name was Butson—volunteered to go into the hole. Butson was lowered slowly at the end of a rope.

Ike Schlossbach lay on his stomach and kept shining his

flashlight as Butson went down into the hole. Suddenly we heard him call, "He's here! He's alive!" Butson was then 110 feet below the surface.

Another rope was quickly lowered. Butson tied it around Peterson's body. We had to pull hard, for Peterson was stuck fast. Slowly he was hauled up out of the hole. Then Butson came up too.

It was then that we found out why Peterson had not taken the knife lowered by Dodson. He had fallen into the crevasse headfirst and was wedged into the hole upside down, with his arms pinned behind his back. His knapsack had fallen forward so that it rested on his head, and the shoulder straps were choking him. Actually, there was no way Peterson could have used the knife, even if he had been able to grab it. So he had gritted his teeth and prepared himself to face a slow death. Peterson had been stuck in the hole upside down for twelve hours before we hauled him up.

Fortunately, he had no broken bones. But the nerves in his arms had been injured because they were pinned against the ice for such a long time. It took several weeks before his arms were normal again.

By the end of July, the sun had begun to return to the Antarctic. We began to prepare for the weeks of exploration during the summer.

Two of the planes had been left aboard the *Beaumont*. There was no room for them at the base camp, and it would have been too difficult to construct hangars to shelter them. Now they were towed off the ship.

Getting the planes ready to fly was a very hard job. It

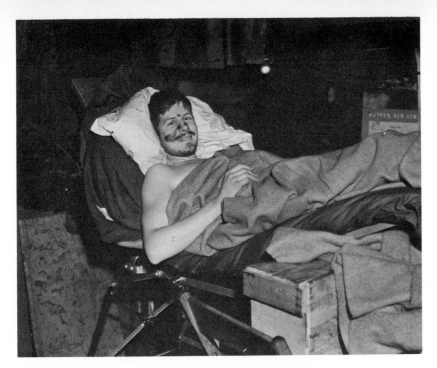

One week after his brush with death, Peterson's face still shows bruises and scabs.

was still bitter cold, but the mechanics could not always wear their heavy work gloves while tuning the engines. Sometimes their skin would stick to the metal, causing painful blisters. Often the engines wouldn't start because the lubricating oil was frozen. The oil had to be heated on the galley stove to thaw it out.

When the engines wouldn't start because of the cold, special heating devices had to be used. Many times the mechanics lost their patience, for it seemed nothing would work. They would thaw the engines with blow torches.

57

In the spring, the two larger planes that had been dismantled and left aboard the *Port of Beaumont* were unloaded. First the twin-engine Beechcraft photography plane was taken off the ship, then the larger Norseman (covered on deck) was removed. Both planes had to be made operational before the air missions could start.

One of the planes was a Norseman, which had one 650-horsepower engine. It had been designed especially for flying in cold weather. The Norseman could haul heavy loads.

The other plane, a Beechcraft with two 450-horsepower engines, had extra radio transmitters. Two additional fuel tanks which had been built-in enabled the plane to fly for nine hours without refueling. The Beechcraft also served as the photography plane. It had trimetrogen cameras mounted inside the fuselage. Only the lenses of the cameras could be seen on the outside.

The idea of trimetrogen cameras was developed during World War II. It is a kind of wide-angle photography. There are three cameras, all electrically operated, which take pictures at the same time. One camera points at a 60-degree angle to the left, another at a 60-degree angle to the right, and the third points straight down. The three cameras cover the terrain below the plane, from one horizon to another.

Spring came. Our two exploration planes were ready to fly. We had come to the great southern continent to explore part of its mysteries. And now we began to do just that.

5

Exploration— Modern Style

In many ways the study of the earth is like solving a great mystery story and jigsaw puzzle combined. Explorers and scientists are the detectives. Bits and pieces of information are collected and fitted together. At last there is a "big picture" containing numerous facts about this planet we call home.

The first pieces were collected by the old-time explorers. Those who blazed the trail into the Antarctic were true heroes. Compared to our modern equipment, the gear they used was pitiful. They had no snow cats, no scientifically designed clothing, no modern trail rations. All they possessed was raw courage and dogged determination. Sometimes they paid with their lives, as they tried to add one more piece of knowledge to the jigsaw puzzle. The English Antarctic explorer Robert Falcon Scott and his heroic men all died on the return trip from the South Pole. Sir Ernest Henry Shackleton, one of the greatest of all Antarctic explorers, came within less than one hundred miles of the South Pole, but had to turn back.

Only someone who has known the terrifying cold, the gnawing hunger of short rations, and the rugged marches through blinding blizzards can appreciate what these giants went through. Those who followed in their footsteps can only salute them.

Now it was our turn to gather information about the Antarctic.

We had already set up another weather station; this time it was established at Cape Keeler. This piece of land is located on the Weddell Sea coast, about 125 miles from Stonington Island. Several drums of gasoline had been stored there. Now, when our planes explored south along the Weddell Sea coast, they would not have to return to Stonington Island to refuel. Instead, they could simply go back up the coastline to Cape Keeler for more gasoline.

But the expedition was not going to depend only on airplanes. There were many things which could not be seen from the air, and many experiments which could be made only on the ground.

For example, one sledge party was going to move south from Stonington Island, and collect all sorts of rock specimens (just as the astronauts did when they landed on the moon). Scientists could study the rocks and determine when the southern end of the earth had begun to cool and form its layer of ice.

At Cape Keeler, an advance supply base across the Palmer Peninsula, gasoline was stored so the men could refuel their planes without having to return to Stonington Island.

They could also learn which minerals were to be found in the Antarctic.

So planes and dog sledges were both important. And, by using modern methods, the pilots and dog drivers would work together. It was the best way to accomplish all our missions.

A kind of hedgehopping system was worked out. The planes would go out first, scouting for safe trails which the dog drivers could use. The dog drivers would follow those trails. Along the way, they would mark good spots for the planes to use as landing strips. Also, the sledgers would leave small caches of emergency supplies along the trails. If the planes met with an accident and were forced down, the men would have emergency food until help came.

The planes could also drop off larger amounts of supplies along the trails taken by the sledgers. These new supply dumps were really advance bases. In that way, the dog teams could move farther and farther toward their next big supply dump. They never had to go back to the main base for more supplies.

It is fine to make plans. But sometimes they do not work. The plans are good, but Mother Nature can upset any schemes.

Bob Nichols, the geologist, left Stonington Island with a small crew and three sledges which carried more than a ton of supplies. Each sledge carried radios, tents, food for a hundred days, sleeping bags, and many other stores.

But summer was coming. The ice of Marguerite Bay was getting thin in spots. The fresh snow that fell turned to slush. Once one of the dog teams fell through the ice. When Nichols tried to drag them back, he fell through the ice too. Tired, bedraggled, unable to go farther, the party turned back to Stonington. They had covered only twenty miles.

At this point Major Butler, the British commander on Stonington Island, proposed that we combine our men and

According to the system of hedgehopping that was worked out, the planes would scout and find safe trails for the dog drivers to use. The dog drivers, in turn, would make landing spots for the planes. Here, at one of these many stopover camps, the planes were anchored to "dead men," and the flight crews slept in tents pitched nearby.

supplies. Perhaps in that way we could put stronger parties in the field. It would be easier to explore the Weddell coastline.

Our expedition had lost quite a few dogs during the distemper epidemic. British dogs and drivers would be useful. So I accepted Major Butler's offer with many thanks. And when the major said that he wanted to be one of the dog drivers, I knew that the party would be in good hands.

So that there would be stronger parties in the field, Major Butler (left) volunteered to combine his men and supplies with those of Commander Ronne.

First, however, we had to ferry a large quantity of supplies over to Cape Keeler. The food and gear would be used by the sledgers from Stonington Island.

Our Norseman plane could do that job easily enough. The British only had one small scout plane, not in the best condition, for its radio was faulty. And that broken radio very nearly meant disaster for the British flyers.

The British plane with three men aboard was supposed to fly ahead and pick out a good landing spot for the larger, heavier Norseman plane. So it took off first and the Norseman followed a few minutes later. But the planes became separated in foul weather. When the Norseman reached Cape Keeler, the British plane was nowhere to be seen. As the weather worsened, the Norseman was forced to turn back, still carrying its supplies. The British plane did not come back.

For eight long days my pilots, Lassiter and Adams, flew search missions. They scoured the plateau for signs of the three missing British airmen. On the ninth day, just as everyone was about to give them up for lost, Lassiter spotted them. They were walking along the sea ice of Marguerite Bay, still forty miles from safety.

We learned that their small plane had landed at Cape Keeler, and when the Norseman didn't show up, the airmen took off to return to their own base. But they got lost in the bad weather. Without a good radio, they were unable to contact anybody. The light plane crash-landed on the ice. The three men weren't hurt, but they had had almost nothing to eat for nine days and were weak and tired.

The American-British Weddell Sea coast party was made up of Major Butler, his aide, Walter Smith, and Eagle Boy Scout Arthur Owen. To prevent their skis and poles from being buried in the snow, they placed them outside their tents in an upright position.

The British-American dog-sledge party which was to explore the Weddell Sea coast had far greater success. I had selected Walter Smith, who had been my chief mate on the *Beaumont,* and Arthur Owen, the Eagle Scout from Texas, to go on the mission. Major Butler and one of his men completed the crew.

The work accomplished by these four men was absolutely magnificent! No—they made no startling discoveries. That happens only in movies, very seldom in true-life exploration. But they worked steadily, making their maps, pressing ahead with quiet determination. At the end of two months, the British pair turned back, for that was part of the plan. Smith and Owen kept on, mapping, collecting rocks, measuring ice thicknesses along the shore. Their journey lasted 106 days, and in that time they covered 1,180 miles.

Throughout the entire sledge trip, these men exactly located mountain peaks and other terrain features. These would tie in with the photographs taken from the air. In that way, by air and on the surface of the frozen wasteland, we could cross-check our maps. They were sure to be accurate.

Walter Smith and Arthur Owen stand in front of a snow cairn they built during their 1,180 mile journey of mapping and exploration. This was the farthest south reached by the Ronne Weddell Sea coast sledge-party before returning to base.

The geologists, Nichols and Dodson, had had bad luck when they tried to sledge out before. But they did much better the next time. They ranged far down the western side of the Palmer Peninsula. We were supposd to supply them by air, but that was not always possible because of bad weather. Once their food almost ran out. The two men were forced to live on a cup of lemonade and a chunk of seal meat per day.

Also, Dodson suffered from a peculiar type of cold-weather illness. The freezing air caused the metal fillings in his teeth to contract. He would be chewing on a mouthful of food and suddenly one of his fillings would plop into his mouth. Soon there wasn't a metal filling left in any of his teeth.

There was only one favor these two men asked of us: that the supply plane take back their sledgeful of rock samples, because the load was becoming too heavy for the Huskies. Then off they went again, collecting still more rock samples, checking maps, pushing farther and farther southward.

On November 4, the heavy clouds which had covered the Palmer Peninsula for so long began to scatter. The photography plane flew to Cape Keeler. Three days later, we began to photograph the great unexplored sections of the Antarctic.

Watching our photographer, Bill Latady, getting ready for a flight was an amusing sight. He wore a special flying suit, which had pockets everywhere, even in the sleeves. Every one of the pockets was crammed full of food. He even took the seat out of his parachute and stuffed it with things to eat.

"Bill," I said, laughing, "if you were forced down, you could live for a whole month on what is in your pockets."

70

Geologists Dodson (left) and Nichols (right) used a hand-crank radio to ask that a plane fly out the rocks they had collected. The weight of the rocks in the fully-loaded sledge was too much for the Huskies to haul.

Our first flight out over the Weddell Sea was a short one. We wanted to get used to the idea of taking pictures and spotting mountains and glaciers from the air. But even that short flight, and the next few brief ones, proved that all the maps of the Antarctic—every last one of them!—would have to be changed a great deal.

Back in 1928, when Sir Hubert Wilkins flew over the same area, he reported seeing some islands east of Cape Keeler. In 1941, when I had flown over that region, I too thought there were islands there. On both flights there were many clouds in the sky.

But now the weather was perfectly clear. Although we flew for almost four hours and could see for miles around, neither I nor anyone else in the plane spotted an island. So it was obvious that on certain days, when clouds formed low over the water, the clouds appeared to be islands. Sir Hubert Wilkins was fooled. So was I. So were several other experienced explorers.

Other short flights showed many more mistakes on the map. One dot of land, which was supposed to be an island, was connected with the mainland by a snow-covered ridge. One bay was twenty miles larger than the map showed. We spotted a new glacier from the air, which was not on any Antarctic map.

But all these short flights, important though they were, only served to train us for the longer flights still to come.

On November 21, the Norseman and the Beechcraft took off from Cape Keeler on our first long flight. The Norseman was carrying extra drums of gasoline, which were to be used by the Beechcraft photography plane later on. When it was time to refuel, both planes were to land near Mount Tricorn, because it was so well marked on all maps.

Ike Schlossback (right), Commander Ronne (left) and Jim Robertson (top) refuel the Norseman plane nicknamed "Nana" (after the North American Newspaper Alliance).

Mount Tricorn came into view, and beyond it stretched the great white unknown. We continued to fly south, with a beautiful mountain range to the right of the plane. Less than an hour later, I spotted a snow-covered mountain, an easily recognizable terrain feature. Lassiter thought it would be a good idea to land near the mountain and refuel.

Mount Tricorn was a distinct landmark that Commander Ronne's planes passed on the flight south. When Ronne took sun observations, he discovered that Mount Tricorn was 55 miles farther north than was shown on the latest maps!

From the air, we couldn't tell how deep the snow was. If it was too deep, the heavy planes might sink down and damage its landing skis or the propeller. But it was a chance we had to take.

Sure enough the snow was deep. But we were lucky, for we stopped without damaging either of the planes. When I leaped out, the snow was up to my waist.

Refueling the photography plane turned out to be a rugged job. Each drum of gasoline weighed 450 pounds. The men and I pushed and pulled and dragged the drums through the deep snow, then we had to pour the gas into a smaller container in order to fill the Beechcraft tanks.

When that job was finished, I began to calculate our exact position. First I took sightings of the sun with a bubble sextant, then I wrote down many numbers—how long we had flown, how far the plane had traveled. But something was wrong. The numbers didn't check out. If my calculations were correct, we weren't supposed to be near Mount Tricorn at all. Yet we had passed it nearly a half hour earlier.

With my pilot, Jim Lassiter, checking all my figures, I started all over again. First the sightings with the bubble sextant, then the calculations based on the plane's odometer and speedometer. I checked my figures against the map. Lassiter and I agreed that my figures were right and the map was wrong!

Mount Tricorn was fifty-five miles farther north than was shown on the latest maps. Also, parts of the Weddell Sea were thirty miles farther west than the maps showed.

Landmarks, such as Mount Tricorn, and all the coast-lines, are extremely important to map makers. They must be plotted accurately, down to the last detail. Why? Well, for example:

Think how mixed up travelers would be if they were told that the Statue of Liberty was in the middle of New Jersey!

Think how confused they would be if they learned that Boston Harbor was off the coast of Maine!

We loaded back aboard the Beechcraft. The Norseman was ordered to stay on the ground. In case something happened to my photography plane, I wanted to have a rescue craft not far away. Besides, gasoline was too precious to be wasted. The Norseman crew would not be helping with the photography, so there was no need for it to fly alongside us.

The Beechcraft skimmed through and over the deep snow, and in a few minutes we were again high in the air. As we flew on, whole groups of mountains came into view, which had never before been seen by human eyes or plotted on any map.

And this is the truly exciting part of modern exploration. No one screams, "Hooray, we have discovered something!" All of us are busy, hastily scribbling notes, plotting things on maps, checking and rechecking to make sure of our figures. Perhaps, to some who like great dramatic adventures, it might seem dull. But to the explorer—whether on the ground, under the sea, or high in space—it is a great, joyous feeling. For we know we have added some little bit of new information to the great jigsaw puzzle.

As we passed the mountains I named them: Sweeney Mountains, Scaife Mountains, Wilkins Mountains, Cape Smith, Lowell Thomas Mountains. I was naming ranges, mountains, glaciers, and capes in honor of members of the expedition and friends who had helped me with money and equipment. Nobody had to give me permission to name those landmarks. That is one of the traditional privileges enjoyed by the commander of any expedition. But all of these newly named features had later to be submitted to the Board of Geographic Names, an official committee in Washington, D.C.

Wilkins Mountains were named by Commander Ronne for Sir Hubert Wilkins, an Australian, one of the great explorers of the Antarctic.

The last mountain I named on that first trip was Mount Hassage, in honor of the fine chief engineer of the *Beaumont*. It was about five thousand feet high. Beyond Mount Hassage, I could see Mount Ulmer, which had been discovered back in 1935 by the American polar explorer Lincoln Ellsworth and named in honor of his wife.

Our flight had proved that the long mountain range running down the middle of the Palmer Peninsula ended in the highlands called the Joerg Plateau. This plateau is about four thousand feet above sea level. And, because our plane was so high up—about ten thousand feet—we could see about two hundred miles beyond the last mountain. Only more uplands could be sighted.

From our position, it seemed clear to both Lassiter and myself that the plateau was connected with the Queen Maud Mountain Range, which lay just southeast of the Ross Ice Shelf. Thus there was no frozen strait from the Ross Sea to the Weddell Sea. Instead, there were highlands, plateaus, and mountains, about four or five thousand feet above sea level.

As far as we could determine, Antarctica was *one continent*.

When we turned to go back, I had Bill Latady drop an American flag onto the snow below. At that time, I also dropped a note in an envelope which claimed this newly discovered land in the name of my adopted country, the United States. Carbon copies of all claim sheets were later deposited with the Department of State in Washington.

6

More Discoveries

It was three weeks before we could leave our base for another flight. Because of the heavy, low clouds, visibility was limited. Even if we had gone aloft we would have seen very little. Also, the snow was slushy. The Norseman could not load too much extra gasoline, for the extra weight would make it too difficult to lift the plane off the ground.

Still, we had to take some risks. The warmer weather in the Antarctic lasts only a few weeks. Once winter returned, flying would be impossible.

As soon as the clouds lifted, both planes were airborne again. Hours later, we spotted the British-American Weddell coast party. They had reached Wright Inlet, hundreds of miles down the east coast of the Palmer Peninsula. When we landed to refuel the Beechcraft, the British pair turned back toward Stonington Island.

The navy does not use flowery speech in order to praise persons who perform their mission with distinction. An admiral or other high officer will merely say, "Well done!" And to those two able Britishers—Major Butler and his aide—I could only say with all my heart, "Well done!"

For two days both planes remained on the ground. High winds, swirling and whipping the snow, swept over our tiny camp. The winds gusted at forty miles an hour, and to have tried a takeoff would have been suicide. In *any* season, Antarctic weather is not to be trusted.

At last the winds died down. Because the Norseman had not been able to carry too much extra fuel, the photography plane (the Beechcraft) would be unable to fly as far as we had hoped. But we took off, determined to map from the air as much unknown territory as possible.

Down the Weddell Sea coast flew the Beechcraft, probing farther south in that area than any man had ever gone. Other explorers had tried to edge south along the Weddell shore, but they had met with disaster. Sir Ernest Shackleton had not succeeded, and neither had the German explorer, Wilhelm Filchner. Both men and their crews had been trapped in the Weddell Sea pack ice. They had drifted northward for months, until they reached open water.

We were the first ones to reach that region and explore it.

Below us stretched a huge ice cliff, rising about 150 feet out of the water. It formed the southernmost boundary of the Weddell Sea, connecting the Palmer Peninsula with Coats

As the twin-engine Beechcraft probed the Weddell Sea coast, areas of land never before seen
by man were photographed with the trimetrogen camera.

Land.

I named the coastline south of Mount Tricorn Lassiter Coast in honor of my good friend and pilot, Jim Lassiter. The other members of my expedition had no cause to be jealous, for they too had landmarks named after them: Latady Mountains, Dodson Island, Gutenko Mountains, Mount Thompson, Cape Schlossbach, Cape Adams. No one was left out.

And still the plane's nose was pointed south as we flew on into the unknown. We could see two hundred miles ahead to the horizon, but no more mountains were visible. On one side of us was a heavy bank of clouds, on the other side was the vast expanse of the Antarctic continent. Below was nothing but ice and snow—and deep, deep silence, broken only by the drone of the engines.

Suddenly, the two engines sputtered, and the plane began to lose altitude. I looked at Lassiter and saw that he was busily working switches on the instrument panel. Seconds later, the engines hummed smoothly again. Jim had switched off his empty gas tanks and switched on the full ones. That accounted for the sputtering.

Once more an American flag was dropped. Also flung from the plane was a claim sheet, which stated that all the land in the area was claimed in the name of the United States. The entire expanse was called Edith Ronne Land in honor of my wife. She had worked with me on the expedition since it was first planned.

When fuel ran low, we returned to Cape Keeler. The Beechcraft had been in the air for twelve-and-a-half hours. As

An aerial view of the route taken by the Ronne Weddell Sea coast party shows newly discovered and named features. This party covered 1,180 miles during 105 days on the trail.

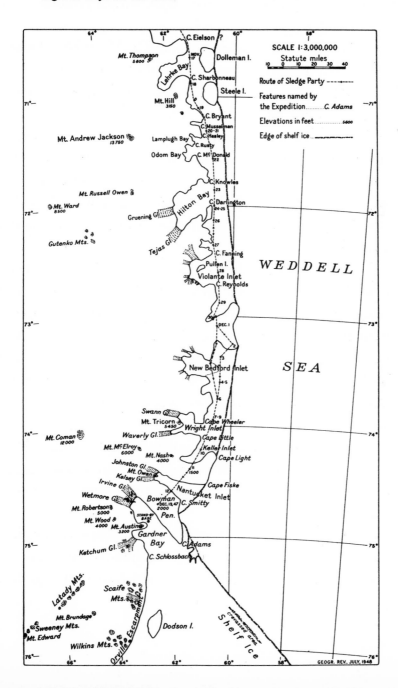

the last drops of spare gasoline were pumped into the tank of the photography plane, I leaned back with a sense of pride and satisfaction.

We had gone where no humans had ever been before. We had seen huge, unknown areas of the Antarctic. Our plane had enabled us to map and explore regions a thousand miles or more from our main base on Stonington Island.

Later, we made a few more short flights, which added much valuable information to the maps of the Antarctic. One such flight took us along the western edge of the Palmer Peninsula. Years before, Carl Eklund and I had sledged along that route. Now I wanted to go farther south than Eklund and I had gone.

About three hundred miles south of Stonington Island, we suddenly lost radio contact with the base. If the plane had developed engine trouble and been forced down, it is almost certain that we would never have been found, at least not alive. The Antarctic is so vast, so remote, so difficult to cross, that search parties would not have been able to find us or reach us. Yet we took that risk. And we even landed the plane twice on purpose.

We had flown over what is now called the Robert English Coast. New mountains were sighted, one of which I named Rex Mountain. That mass of rock and snow rises to a height of six thousand feet.

In order to plot the location accurately, it was necessary to land. I had to take a position sight with the sextant while on the ground. We landed all right, and I took the sighting. But,

84

while moving back to the plane, I suddenly realized the dangerous position we were in.

Suppose the landing ski had broken?

Suppose the snow was too deep to allow the plane to get back into the air?

Suppose suddenly the engine conked out?

We had no radio contact. Where would a search party have begun to look for us?

Even Jim Lassiter, who is usually very calm, seemed to be quite nervous. "Hurry up, Commander," he called out sharply. "Let's get back into the air where it's safe!"

On the return trip, we made a more accurate map of the west coast of Alexander Island. Off in the distance was Charcot Island, first sighted from the sea in 1909 by the French explorer Jean Baptiste Charcot. Nobody had ever set foot on that island. Lassiter, Latady, and I wanted to land there to determine the exact position of the three mountain peaks on the north side of the island. This was the second time we landed the plane on purpose. I took a few altitude shots of the sun and figured out the exact longitude of our landing spot. Not far off were the three sharp mountain peaks. Otherwise the rest of the island was flat and snow covered.

Suddenly dark clouds began to form swiftly. We were afraid that the bad weather was mostly over Stonington Island. The Beechcraft took off, and when we came into radio range once more, we called the base to ask about weather conditions. Our worst fears were realized. A seventy-mile-an-hour gale was whipping at the base. If we tried to land there, the

85

On the return trip, Commander Ronne made a more
accurate map of the west coast of Alexander Island.
Also visible on this map are weather stations and the
routes of trail parties.

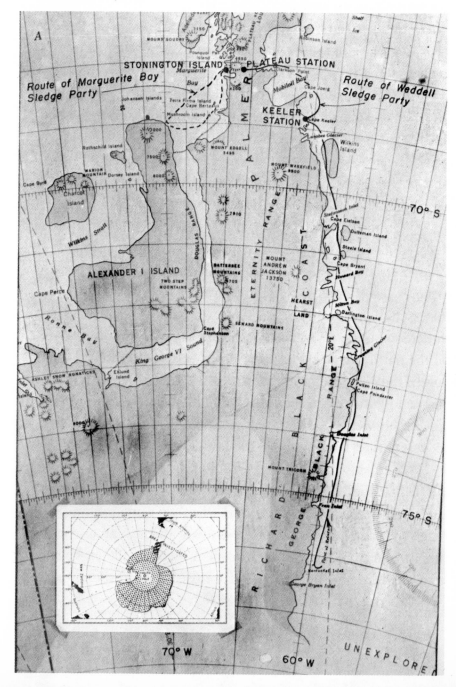

wind would very likely flip the plane over.

At first I thought about landing along George VI Sound and staying there until the storm died down. Then I realized that wasn't such a good idea. We might have to stay there for a long time, and we didn't have enough food to last more than a week or so.

"Commander, let's make a run for home," said Jim Lassiter.

"We'll try that, Jim." I told him. "Do your best."

In order to see where he was flying, Lassiter had to keep the plane under the dark, threatening clouds. At first the Beechcraft flew at about three thousand feet, but as the clouds kept dropping lower, he had to cut his altitude too. When we were still about fifty miles from camp, he dropped to four hundred feet, then to three hundred feet, and to two hundred feet.

We skimmed over icebergs floating in the open water off the coast. Once, when a sudden downdraft caught the plane, the plotting board and map which lay across my lap flew up and hit me in the face. The Beechcraft snapped down to within a few feet of the water before Lassiter managed to steady it. We could see the white tops of the waves below—so close that we could almost reach out and touch them. I thought surly this was the end for Lassiter, Latady, and me.

Somehow, Lassiter held the plane level, and then he began to inch up again. He was magnificent as he kept veering away from icebergs, zigzagging between them, and fighting winds which buffeted the plane. The base radio operator told us that the winds were getting stronger.

At last Lassiter spotted some smooth sea ice down below. We were over Neny Fjord, which is a section of Marguerite Bay. Slowly Lassiter inched the plane down to a landing, only two miles from camp.

A tractor was sent out to haul the plane back. But it wasn't an easy trip. Two men had to lie flat on each wing to break the air flow. Otherwise the plane would have risen up and sailed away like a kite.

Our exploration of the Palmer Peninsula was now officially finished. To celebrate, we had a fine party.

On January 22, my Weddell Sea coast group returned to Stonington Island. Everyone was back and in good health.

It was time to leave the Antarctic. The men began to pack the gear, take the wings off the planes, and move all our equipment back to the *Beaumont*. On February 11, 1948, we received a radio message from a United States Navy icebreaker. The captain was an old friend, and he wanted to pay us a visit. He also offered to break the ice around our ship so that we could follow in his wake to the open water.

When the last bit of gear had been stowed aboard the *Beaumont*, we entered the final words in the expedition's log. We had completed all our missions successfully. And the Ronne Antarctic Research Expedition had added much useful knowledge to man's understanding of the universe.

By land and air, we had explored and mapped more than 450,000 square miles of new territory. More than half of that area had never before been seen by human eye. Much of the rest had never been properly mapped.

The planes flew a total of forty thousand miles.

The *Port of Beaumont* at winter quarters. This was the first time in history that a diesel-driven ship had intentionally been frozen into the Antarctic ice for the winter. By the time Commander Ronne's friends on the two Navy icebreakers paid him a visit, the sun's intense heat had pretty well melted and broken up the ice floes. With the icebreakers pushing aside the remaining ice, the Ronne Antarctic Research Expedition followed them to the open sea.

Bill Latady took more than fourteen thousand aerial photographs.

Perhaps the area we covered might be easier to picture if it is compared with the same area in the United States:

If the main base had been located at New York City (instead of Stonington Island), I would have been sending the dog teams as faraway as the state of Ohio!

My planes would have been flying as far south as the state of Florida!

And we would have sighted and mapped an area equal to the states of New York, New Jersey, Pennsylvania, Ohio, Michigan, Maryland, Virginia, West Virginia, North Carolina, South Carolina, Georgia, and the northern edge of Florida!

The scientists in the expedition had worked very hard, and I was proud of their accomplishments. They performed experiments in eleven branches of science and wrote fourteen reports.

Thompson's main interest had been to record earthquakes. His instruments were so sensitive that they could detect disturbances all over the world. But he also did valuable research on magnetism. He learned much about the Antarctic tides, about which little had been known before.

Peterson had sent weather information to Washington by radio twice a day. He also studied cosmic rays and the sun's radiation during Antarctic summer. Moisture normally blocks the sun's rays. Peterson learned that since the cold Antarctic air holds little moisture, radiation there is less weakened by clouds than we had expected.

90

More geological research than ever before was done by Nichols and Dodson. They found traces of many minerals, including iron, copper, gold, and silver. But the ore was of a low grade and not very valuable. According to their Geiger counter, there were no traces of radium.

We sailed from Stonington Island at the end of February. It was thirteen months after the *Beaumont* had left Texas. All about us ice floes were once more beginning to choke the bay. Soon it would be Antarctic winter again, and the seas around the Palmer Peninsula would be sealed shut by pack ice.

We sailed steadily northward. Before long the great ice cliffs of the Antarctic had disappeared from view beyond the southern horizon.

In my heart I knew that some day I would return to Antarctica, with a new expedition. And I did. I was fortunate enough to head the American base at the Weddell Sea during the International Geophysical Year (1957–59). And in 1961, I finally set foot at the South Pole on the fiftieth anniversary of its discovery by the master explorer, Roald Amundsen.

FINN RONNE, who was born in Horten, Norway, grew up in a household of tales of sea and of exploration. His father, Martin Ronne, was the companion of Roald Amundsen, a great Norwegian polar explorer, and often took his son to the docks to watch Amundsen's ship *Fram* being outfitted.

Although Finn often dreamed of the time he too would sail to distant lands, he busied himself with school and athletics. He learned to ski, participated in gymnastics, soccer, football, swimming, and mountain climbing. Hiking, camping, and sailing were also regular weekend sports. From his special hobby, collecting stamps, Finn developed a keen interest in geography that reinforced his already full-blown desire to explore.

At Horten Technical College, Ronne studied marine engineering and naval architecture before coming to the United States in 1923. Six years later, he became a naturalized citizen. In 1933, his childhood dream of exploring was realized when he accompanied Admiral Richard E. Byrd to Antarctica. Since then, on his own and with the U.S. Navy, Ronne has made thirteen trips of exploration to polar regions, and has been awarded numerous honors. His expedition of 1946–48, about which this book is written, was the last private American expedition to venture into the Antarctic. Ronne served in the U.S. Navy until 1961 when he retired with the rank of Captain.

Today, Captain Finn Ronne makes his home in Washington, D.C., and lectures as well as writes about his polar adventures.

92

Index

A

Adams, Charles, 22, 67
Air, currents, measurement of, 39
Airplanes, 17, 18, 20, 22, 37, 49, 54, 56, 62, 63-64, 70, 85-88. *See also* individual planes
Alexander Land, 10, 11, 85
Amundsen, Roald, 91
Andes Mountains, 16
Antarctic, early explorations of, 10-11, 61-62; geography of, 14-17, 30-32, 46-47; climate of, 25-27, 34; Ronne's exploration of, 70-78, 79-91
Appetite, effects of cold on, 41-44
Arctic, the, 21, 26
Argentina, 34
Army, United States, 27, 39
Astronauts, 62
Atlantic Ocean, 10, 30
Australia, 46
Avalanches, 51

B

Bacon fat, 42
Balloons, 39, 50
Barley, 42
Base camp, 32-34, 35-36, 37, 44, 49. *See also* Stonington Island
Beaumont, Texas, 22-24, 56
Beechcraft, the, 60, 70-78, 79-84, 85-88
Bellingshausen, Fabian Von, 10
Bellingshausen Sea, 10, 14
Blizzards, 14, 34, 49, 51-52, 54-55, 62
Boston Harbor, 76
Butler, Major, 34, 64-66, 68, 80
Butson, 55-56

C

Cameras, trimetrogen, 60
Cape Adams, 82
Cape Horn, 14, 16
Cape Keeler, 62, 67, 70, 72, 82-84
Cape Schlossbach, 82
Cape Smith, 77
Carbohydrates, 42, 44
Charcot, Jean Baptiste, 85
Charcot Island, 85
Chile, 24, 34
Chocolates, 43, 44
Climate, 25-27. *See also* Weather
Clothing, 19, 39, 61
Coal, 19
Coats Land, 80-82
Cold. *See* Weather
Compasses, 19
Congress, United States, 20
Cookies, 43
Cooking gear, 19
Cosmic rays, 90
Crevasses, 25, 27-29, 51, 54-56

D

Dangers, Antarctic, 25-30
Darlington, Harry, 22, 37
Darlington, Jennie, 24, 49
"Dead men," 28
Department of State, 78
Distemper epidemic, 30-31, 66
Dodson, Bob, 22, 39, 50, 53, 54-56, 70, 91
Dodson Island, 82
"Dog food," 43
Dogs. *See* Huskies

Byrd, Admiral Richard E., 11-13, 26-27

E

Earth, the, 9, 13, 61
Earthquakes, 9, 39, 90
Eklund, Carl, 11, 28-29, 84
Eklund Island, 11
Ellsworth, Lincoln, 78
England, 34
Equipment, 17-20, 32, 35-39, 44, 47-49, 61, 64, 66-67, 88
Experiments, scientific, 37-39, 47-49, 62-64, 68-70, 88-91

F

Fat, importance of, 41, 44
Filchner, Wilhelm, 80
Finances, 17-18, 20
Food, trail, 19, 37, 41-44, 50, 61, 62, 64, 67, 70, 87

G

Gasoline, 19, 62, 73, 75, 76, 79, 84
Geiger counter, 91
Geographic Names, Board of, 77
Geophysical Year (1957-59), 91
George VI Sound, 11, 37, 47, 87
Glaciers, 32, 72, 77
Graphite, 41
Greenland, 22
Gutenko, Sig, 22, 44
Gutenko Mountains, 82

H

Hassage, Charles, 22
Hedgehopping, system of, 64
Huskies, 19, 28-29, 30, 36, 37, 41, 42-43, 50-51, 52, 55, 64, 68

I

Ice, 9, 10, 11, 16, 27, 28, 30-32, 39-40, 47, 64, 67, 80, 82, 88;
    cliffs, 32, 39-40, 80-82
    floes, 16, 91
    pack, 16, 80

Icebergs, 32, 37, 87
Icebreakers, navy, 16, 88
International Falls, Minnesota, 47

J

Joerg Plateau, 78

K

Kerosene, 42

L

Lassiter, Jim, 22, 67, 74-75, 78, 80-82, 84-88
Lassiter Coast, 82
Latady, Bill, 22, 49, 70-71, 78, 85, 90
Latady Mountains, 82
LeMay, General Curtis, 20
Letter-writing, 24
Library (Expeditions), 49
Lights, southern, 46-47
Little America, (Byrd's camp), 11-13
Log, keeping of, 47-49
Lowell Thomas Mountains, 77

Mc

McClary, Nelson, 39-41
McLean, Doc, 22

M

Machinery, 18
Magnetic fields, 39, 90
Maine, 76
"Man food," 42
Maps and mapping, 11, 17, 69-70, 72, 75-78, 80-82, 84-85, 87, 88-90
Marguerite Bay, 32, 64, 67, 88
Meat, 41, 42, 43, 44
Medical supplies, 19
Minerals, 42, 63, 91
Mirages, 29

Moon, 62
Mount Hassage, 78
Mount Nilsen, 13
Mount Thompson, 82
Mount Tricorn, 74-76, 82
Mount Ulmer, 78

N

Navy, United States, 13, 20, 21, 22, 80, 88
Neny Fjord, 88
New Jersey, 76
Newspaper syndicates, 20
Nichols, Bob, 22, 64, 70, 91
Norseman, the, 60, 67, 72-78, 79-80
North America, 46
North Pole, 26
Northern Hemisphere, 46

O

Organizations, private, 13, 20
Owen, Arthur, 22-24, 68-69

P

Pacific Ocean, 10, 30
Palmer Mountains, 16, 49
Palmer Peninsula, 11, 14, 16-17, 28, 32, 34, 37, 49-50, 70, 78, 79, 80-82, 84, 88, 91
Panama Canal, 24, 30
Panic, problems of, 30
Parkas, fur, 39
Pemmican, 42. *See Also* Food, trail
Penguins, 9
Peterson, Harries-Clichy, 22, 39, 50, 53, 54-56
Photography, 18-19, 22, 60, 69, 70, 73, 84, 90
Port of Beaumont, Texas, the 23-24, 30-32, 36, 37, 41, 56, 78, 88, 91
Primus stoves, 42
Protein, 42

Q

Queen Maud Mountain Range, 78

R

Radiation, 90
Radios, 18, 19, 41, 49, 50, 64, 67, 85, 87, 90
Radio stations, 39-41
Radium, 91
Records, keeping of, 24, 47
Rex Mountain, 84
Robert English Coast, 84-85
Robertson, Jim, 22, 40-41
Rockefeller Mountains, 13
Rocks, specimens of, 9, 62, 68, 70, 91
Ronne Antarct⁻ Research Expedition, 1᠎; mission of, 16-17; equipment for, 17-20, 25; selecting men for, 20-24; challenges and dangers of, 25-30; first arrival in Antarctic, 31-34; preparation of camp and, 35-44; during winter's night, 46-60; and Antarctic explorations, 61-78; accomplishment of mission, 78; discoveries and results of, 79-84, 85-88, 88-91
Ronne Bay, 11
Ronne, Edith (Jackie), 24, 47-49
Ronne Land, Edith, 82
Ross Ice Shelf, 78
Ross Sea, 10, 78
Russia, 10, 11

S

Scaife Mountains, 77
Schlossbach, Isaac (Ike), 21-22, 55-56

Scientific equipment. *See* individual items
Scott, Robert Falcon, 61-62
Scout plane, 37, 53-54, 67
Seals, 9, 41, 43
Seasons, 14, 34, 35, 37, 44, 46-47, 56, 79, 80, 91
Seismographs, 47
Shackleton, Sir Ernest Henry, 62, 80
Ships, 17, 20, 21, 23
Skis, 19, 27, 51, 53, 54, 55, 75, 85
Sledges and sledging, 19, 26-27, 28, 29, 37, 49, 50-51, 52, 54, 62-64, 68-70, 84
Sleeping bags, 19, 39, 64
Smith, Walter, 22, 68-69
Snow, 27, 28, 29-30, 32, 34, 41, 51-52, 53-54, 61, 64, 75, 76, 80, 82, 84, 85
Snow cats, 17, 61
South America, 14, 16, 46
South Pole, 62, 91
Southern Hemisphere, 46
Soy meal, 42
Starch, 44
Statue of Liberty, 76
Stonington Island, 32-34, 37, 47, 49, 53-54, 55, 62, 64, 67, 79, 84, 85, 88, 90, 91
Storms 14, 49
Stoves, 19, 42
Submarine expedition, 21
Sugar, 44
Supplies. *See* Equipment
Supply base, advance, 49, 64, 67
Surplus stores, government, 19-20
Sweeney Mountains, 77

T

Tea, 43
Teeth, disease of, 70
Temperatures, 9, 26-27, 37, 47

Tents, 19, 39, 50, 51, 52, 54, 64
Texas, 22, 68, 91
Thompson, Andrew, 22, 37, 47, 90
Tides, 9, 39, 47
Tractors, 13, 19, 41
Truman, President Harry, 20

U

United States Antarctic Expedition of 1939-41, 10-11, 21-22, 32-33
United States of America, 10-13, 17-18, 34, 47, 78, 82, 90, 91

V

Vitamins, 42

W

Warehouses, military, 19
Washington, D.C., 77, 78
Weather, 14, 21, 25-27, 34, 35, 37, 41, 44, 46-47, 49, 50, 51-54, 57, 60, 62, 67, 70, 72, 79, 85-88
Weather Bureau, United States, 20
Weather station, 39, 49-54, 62
Weddell Sea, 10, 14-17, 49, 62, 88, 91; exploration of coast, 65-66, 68-70, 75, 78, 79-82, 88
Wheat germ, 42
Whiteouts, 25, 29-30
Wilkins Mountains, 77
Wilkins, Sir Hubert, 21, 72
Winds, 26-27, 34, 47, 51, 52, 53, 54, 80; gales, 85-87
Winter night, 34, 46-60
Wright Inlet, 79
World War II, 9-10, 13, 19, 20, 22, 60